Hacking

The Ultimate Beginners Guide

By Max Green

Table of Contents

Introduction

I want to thank you and congratulate you for downloading the book, *"Hacking: The Ultimate Beginner's Guide."*

This book contains proven steps and strategies on how to hack computer networks.

This eBook will teach you the basic concepts used in hacking computers. By reading this book, you will learn the different stages of hacking attacks and the usual terms used by hackers. In addition, you will learn how to gather information about the computers or systems you want to attack. Lastly, you will learn how to crack passwords, hack wireless connections, and install different malwares.

Thanks again for downloading this book, I hope you enjoy it!

Chapter 1: Hacking – The Basics

For many people, hackers possess amazing skills and knowledge that can be used to access information systems and gather important data. The word "hacker" creates a vision of a teenage geek who enters some commands into his computer – and BAM! His device gives out confidential information such as passwords and account numbers. In the real world, a hacker simply needs to know how computer systems work and identify the tools that can be used to find security weaknesses. In this book, you will learn about the tools and techniques being used by professional hackers in attacking computer systems and gathering valuable information.

The world of hackers and how they work is a mystery to many security and computer experts. In general, hackers employ special software tools to collect digital info. By acquiring the same technical skills and using the same tools utilized by hackers, you can defend your computer systems and networks from mischievous attacks.

This chapter will introduce you to the "Hackers' World" and teach you the terms used in discussing digital security. Before you can defend against "evil" hackers, you have to understand various hacking techniques. This book aims to teach you the skills and tools used by hacking experts so that you can use them yourself. Also, this book will help you to become a "white hat hacker." That means you will be one of the "good guys" in the hacking world.

Three Types of Hackers

White Hat Hackers – These are the nice guys: the people who consider ethics whenever they apply their hacking skills. In general, these hackers are employed as security professionals. They use their hacking skills to identify weaknesses in a computer system and prepare countermeasures. Additionally, white hat hackers are the prime candidates for certification exams.

Before applying their tools and knowledge, "white hats" get the permission from the owner of the computer system. Acquiring permission prior to hacking any system is extremely important – it separates security professionals from malicious hackers.

Black Hat Hackers – These hackers are referred to as the bad guys: they use their skills for malicious or illegal purposes. They force their way into remote computer systems with bad intentions. Once they have hacked a system, "black hats" will remove important data, prevent legitimate users from accessing the system, and cause various problems for the owners of the data.

You can easily differentiate black hats from the white hats – black hat hackers have malicious intentions when accessing an account. This is how most people define hackers.

Gray Hat Hackers – These hackers may work defensively or offensively, depending on the scenario. This category is the dividing line between white hats and black hats. Basically, gray hats can be individuals who want to know how to hack but don't intend to use the knowledge for illegal purposes. These hackers claim that they consider ethics as an important factor when using their skills. They learned how to hack out of curiosity.

Gray hats can help system owners in improving their security features. By attacking a system, these hackers can identify a system's vulnerable spots. Afterward, they will share the information with the developers or managers of the computer system.

The Skillset of a Hacker

As a hacker, you should be familiar with computer-related topics such as networking, programming, and operating systems. You also need to master the most popular platforms (Unix, Linux, Windows, etc.). Because of the concentration level and amount of time involved in hacking, you must be patient, persistent, and perseverant.

Most hackers are knowledgeable about computers, programming, networking, and database management. Hackers are often hired as computer security experts – they find the weaknesses of any system using their tools and skills. In general, a hacker must know how to breach security systems: he/she doesn't need to know how to prevent or stop hacking attacks.

The Terms Used in Hacking

If you want to be a hacker, you should be familiar with the terms used by computer experts. Once you understand the language used by hackers, you are one step closer to joining their world. This section of the book will help you to develop your "hacking vocabulary."

- _Exploit_ – This is a tool or technology that abuses glitches, bugs, and system vulnerabilities. Exploit often leads to denial of service, escalation of privileges, and unauthorized access. Black hat hackers start their attack by searching for exploits in the computer system they are targeting.

  In general, exploits are short strings of code that, when entered into a computer system, exposes weaknesses. An experienced hacker can easily create his/her own exploits, but advanced programming skills is not required since there are lots of software programs created for hacking purposes. These computer programs have "precooked" exploits that can be used to attack computer networks or systems. For some hackers, an exploit is a specific method to break into a computer system through its own weaknesses.

- *Threat* – This is a situation or environment that can lead to a possible violation of digital security. Hackers search for threats whenever they perform a security analysis. A hacker's techniques and computer programs are themselves threats to the information security of an organization.

- *Vulnerability* – This refers to an error in logic design, software creation, or program implementation that can result to undesirable and unexpected events (e.g. system damages caused by bad instructions). Hackers use an exploit code to target a system's vulnerability. Once a fault is created or identified, the hacker will be able to acquire valuable information.

- *TOE (Target of Evaluation)* - This is a network, system, or program that is the focus of a hacking attack or security analysis. Hackers are often working on important TOEs, computer systems that hold confidential information like passwords, account numbers, and Social Security numbers. The goal of a hacker is to use his tools and techniques against an important TOE to identify the vulnerabilities and fix them. Thus, they prevent unauthorized access to confidential data.

- *Attack* – This happens when a system or network is compromised through its vulnerabilities. In general, attacks are performed using exploits. Hackers utilize tools to discover computer systems that are prone to an exploit because of its network configuration or operating system.

How Are Exploits Delivered to a Computer System?

You can send exploits in two different ways. These are:

1. _Remote_ –With this method, the exploit is sent through a computer network. It allows hackers to attack a computer system even if they don't have direct access to their target. In general, attacks that are initiated outside the targeted network or system are considered remote.

   People imagine this type of attack whenever they think about hackers. In the real world, however, most hacking attacks fall under the next type.

2. _Local_ – Here, the exploit is sent straight to the targeted network or system. Hackers can only use this method if they have prior access to the target. To prevent this type of attack, system and network owners create IT security regulations that provide each legitimate user with the minimum degree of access to do his/her job function. Thus, users cannot view or modify information that is irrelevant to their tasks.

   The strategy outlined above, sometimes called "least privilege" or "need to access," can prevent local delivery of exploits. It is important to note that most hacking attacks are "internal" (i.e. they are performed by people who belong to the organization). Before an insider can launch an attack, he/she should possess sufficient access to the confidential data. You can accomplish this by escalating the privileges given to you or exploiting the system's weaknesses.

Chapter 2: How to Hack Computer Systems and Networks

According to IT experts, the process of hacking has 5 distinct stages. All hackers (i.e. white hats, black hats, and gray hats) follow these steps. Thus, you have to understand each stage completely if you want to be a great hacker (regardless of the "color" you are aiming for). These stages are:

1. Reconnaissance – In this stage, the hacker gathers information about his/her target. This is divided into two types:

    a. Passive Reconnaissance – Here, you will gather information without the knowledge of your target. This form of reconnaissance can be as plain as observing an office to determine what time employees enter or exit it. However, information gathering for hacking purposes is often conducted in front of a computer.

        You can gather information quickly and easily if you will use the internet. Actually, hackers usually run an online search about the company or organization they are going to attack. You can utilize the power of search engines (e.g. Google, Yahoo!, Bing, etc.) to get the data you need.

You may also use the technique called "sniffing the network" to get technical information such as hidden networks or servers, naming conventions, and IP addresses. This method is similar to office monitoring: the hacker observes the flow of information to determine when transactions occur and where the pieces of data are sent to.

b. Active Reconnaissance – In this type, you will probe the computer network to find services, IP addresses, and individual hosts linked to it. Active reconnaissance employs aggressive techniques. Thus, it involves higher risks of being detected than the passive type.

This way of gathering information can generate important data (e.g. the security measures being used). However, it can also increase the chances of being caught.

Both types of reconnaissance can result to the collection of confidential data. For instance, it's often easy to discover the kind of web server and OS (operating system) the target organization is using. You can use this data to find the vulnerabilities of your target.

2. Scanning – In this stage, you will use the information you have gathered to analyze your target. Here are some of the tools used by hackers in the hacking stage:

   a. Dialer

   b. Port scanner

   c. ICMP (Internet Control Message Protocol) scanner

   d. Network mapper

   e. Ping sweep

f. SNMP (Simple Network Management Protocol) sweeper

g. Vulnerability scanner

Hackers search for the following pieces of information:

i. User accounts

ii. Installed software

iii. Computer names

iv. IP addresses

v. Operating System

3. Getting Access – This is where the actual hacking takes place. The weaknesses discovered during the previous stages are now used to access the target. The attack can be sent

to the target system using a LAN (local area network), local access to a computer, the internet, or offline. Here are some examples: session hijacking, denial of service, and buffer overflows.

This stage is also called "owning the system" because once the target has been hacked; the attackers can control the system as they wish.

4. Maintaining Access – After establishing the connection, the hacker needs to maintain that access for future attacks and exploitations. In some cases, hackers fortify the target using rootkits, backdoors, and Trojans. They do this to secure an exclusive access to the target and prevent security personnel or other hackers from discovering the vulnerabilities being used.

Once the system is hacked, the hacker can use it to launch other attacks. This strategy is called the "zombie system" – the system is forced to hack other targets.

5. Covering the Tracks – Once the hacker has gained and secured access, he/she can cover his/her tracks to:

a. Prevent detection by IT personnel

b. Remove evidence of their hacking activities

c. Avoid legal action

d. Continue using the hacked system.

In general, hackers want to eliminate all traces of their attack like log files and IDS (intrusion detection system) alarms. Here are some of the things they do to cover their tracks:

i. Modifying the log files

ii. Steganography

iii. Employing a tunneling protocol

The Technology Used by Hackers

Nowadays, there are many tools and methods that you can use to locate weaknesses, run exploits, and attack targets. After finding the vulnerabilities of a system, you may start your attack and install malware (i.e. malicious software). Here are some types of malware: backdoors, rootkits, and Trojans.

SQL injection and buffer overflows are two other techniques used to access computer networks. In general, these techniques are employed when attacking databases and application servers.

Hacking tools are used to exploit one of these areas:

- *Applications* – Often, applications are not checked for weaknesses: programmers don't test their projects during the Code Writing phase. That means any application may have programming errors that you can take advantage of. Basically, the process of creating an application is driven by features – the programmers need to create the most feature-rich version of their project in the shortest period of time.

- *Misconfigurations* – In some cases, computer systems have erroneous setups. Hackers can take advantage of this by discovering those errors and making sure that they won't be detected or corrected by the security personnel.

- *Shrink-Wrap Code* – Lots of ready-made computer programs have bonus features the average user doesn't know about. You can use these features to breach a network's defenses. For instance, Microsoft Word has the "macros" feature – hackers can use this to trigger programs inside the application.

- *Operating Systems* – Most system administrators apply the default settings when installing new operating systems. Since the default settings are not designed to prevent network attacks, a hacker may find a vulnerability that can be exploited.

Different Types of Hacking Attacks

Hackers employ a wide range of techniques to overcome the target's defenses. In general, hackers try to specialize in two to four hacking techniques. This allows them to have an in-depth knowledge about the attacking method they want to use. Hacking methods are extremely complex: it would be hard and impractical if you will try to master all of them.

When talking to a client, a hacker asks whether there are particular problem areas like social engineering or wireless networks. This information can help the hacker in customizing his attack.

The following list shows the most popular entry points for hacking attacks:

- Local Network – A LAN (Local Area Network) attack simulates a person who wants to gain EXTRA and UNAUTHORIZED access to a local network. Here, the hacker should establish access to the network before he can launch this attack.

   WLANs (Wireless LANs) belong to this category and provide an extra entry point for hackers as the radio waves pass through solid structures. Since WLAN signals can be determined and tapped outside the building, attackers don't have to access the computer network physically and execute the hacking procedure. In addition, the growing popularity of WLANs has turned this method into a go-to trick for black hat hackers.

- Remote Network – Remote network hacks try to simulate an outsider attacking the system through the internet. The hacker attempts to breach or discover weaknesses in the external defenses of the target (e.g. proxy, router, or firewall vulnerabilities). The internet is considered as the most popular hacking instrument. Because of this, many technology-intensive organizations have fortified their defenses against "online hackers."

- Stolen Equipment – Here, the hacker steals a data resource owned by a member of the target organization (e.g. employee). Data such as passwords, usernames, encryption types and security settings can be acquired by stealing a physical device (e.g. laptop, desktop, smartphone, tablet, etc.). This area is usually overlooked by lots of organizations: they focus too much on the electronic side of things.

Once hackers gain access to a device authorized by the security domain, many types of information (e.g. security settings) can be obtained. When a laptop disappears, the owner doesn't report it immediately since he/she thinks that the loss is a personal one. This way of thinking is incorrect. Stolen devices must be reported as soon as possible so that the security personnel can prevent the missing gadget from accessing the network. If the owner retrieves the device, he/she can just contact the system administrator to have it unlocked.

- Remote Dial-Up Network – Here, the hacker launches an attack against the target's modem pools. For instance, hackers use war dialing (i.e. the process of dialing repeatedly to discover system vulnerabilities) in violating the defenses of a dial-up network. To prevent this hacking method, lots of organizations have replaced dial-up connections with secure internet connections.

- Social Engineering – With this point of attack, the hacker tries to exploit the integrity and security of the network's authorized members. Hackers who use social engineering employ face-to-face or telephone communication to get the information they need. You can use social engineering to obtain passwords, usernames, and other security measures of the target.

- Physical Entry – This point of attack refers to the target's physical premises. A hacker who obtains physical access to a network can plant rootkits, Trojans, viruses, or key loggers (a device that can record keystrokes). In addition, the hacker may gather confidential files that are not placed in secure locations. Finally, an intruder who gets physical access to the target's building may install rogue gadgets such as wireless access points. A wireless access point allows a hacker to access the local network even if he/she is in a remote location.

Chapter 3: How to Gather Data About Your Target

Before you can hack any target, you should have enough information about it. Gathering information, also called footprinting, is the act of collecting information related to the target. This process is now easy and simple, thanks to the internet and powerful search engines. All you need to do is access your favorite search engine (e.g. Google), enter some keywords, and BAM! You will get thousands of webpages containing information about the words you searched for.

This chapter will teach you some techniques used to obtain information. Study this carefully since it can help you become a good hacker.

Reconnaissance

This is a catchall word for observing the target and collecting information regarding where, how, and when they do things. By determining behavioral patterns, of the entire system or its members, a hacker can discover and use a loophole.

Competitive Intelligence

Competitive intelligence refers to the data about the products, services, technologies, and strategies being used by an organization's competitor. Almost all forms of competitive intelligence are benign in nature and don't affect the organization being targeted. This method of information gathering is used to simply monitor how competitors are marketing their services or products.

In this section, you will learn how to use Spy Fu. SpyFu is an online hacking tool that can determine the keywords used for websites. Since it is 100% passive, your targets won't notice that you are obtaining data about them.

How to Use SpyFu

- Pull up a web browser and go to the SpyFu website (i.e. www.spyfu.com).

- Type in the web address of your target inside the search box.

- Read the report and identify important links, keywords, or other types of information.

How to Use the EDGAR Database

If you are going to hack a large corporation, you need to use the EDGAR database. This database contains information about public companies (i.e. those that are being traded in the stock market). You can get valuable information by checking the SEC filings for addresses and contact names. Here's what you need to do:

1. Use Google to identify the stock symbol of your target (e.g. DIS for Disney, AMZN for Amazon, etc.).

2. Go to the SEC website: www.sec.gov.

3. Click on the link that says EDGAR Filers. You'll find this link on the right-hand side of the webpage.

4. Click on the link that says "Search for Filings" and type in the stock symbol of your target. Through this method, you will learn valuable information such as where the corporation got registered and who filed the documents for it.

5. Visit Yahoo!'s yellow pages (http://yp.yahoo.com) to check if a phone number or physical address is

entered for any of the names you will find in the EDGAR database.

More Details About Footprinting

Footprinting is the process of generating a map or blueprint of an organization's information system. The footprinting process starts by identifying the system, application, or location of the organization being targeted. Once this information is obtained, the hacker may collect specific details about the target through nonintrusive techniques. For instance, the target's own website may provide a directory of its personnel. Information about an organization's employees can be used to conduct social engineering tactics.

The Tools That You Can Use in Footprinting

You can footprint your targets using different tools, either websites or applications, which allow you to search for data passively. Through these footprinting tools, you may obtain valuable information about their target. By footprinting your target, you can eliminate the hacking tools that you cannot use.

For instance, if you are attacking an organization that uses Windows computers, you may eliminate your hacking tools that target Macintosh systems. Thus, footprinting gives you two advantages: (1) it improves the efficiency of the hacking procedure and (2) it reduces the possibility of detection since you will be using the best tools for the hacking activity.

Here are the common tools used by hackers during the information gathering stage:

- Whois – This tool was originally developed for the operating system called Unix. Nowadays, it can be found online, in hacking toolkits, and other operating systems. Basically, Whois determines the registered person for any domain name.

    How to Use this Tool:

    - Access DNSStuff (www.dnsstuff.com) and look for the free tools. You'll find them at the bottom of the webpage.

    - Enter the URL of your target inside the WHOIS Lookup search box. Then, click on the button that says "WHOIS."

- Read the results and identify the following:

    - Contact email

    - Registered address

    - DNS and Technical Contacts

    - Expiration Date

    - Phone number

- Access your target's website and verify if the contact information you gathered from the previous steps are correct.

- If the information you have matches the data listed on the target's website, run a Google search for the email addresses or names of employees. Using this technique, you will know the naming convention used by the organization in creating email addresses for its members.

- Packet-Tracking Tools – These tools allow you to determine the path of data packets inside the target network. Also, they can help you identify the physical location of the target's routers and internet-related devices. In general, packet-tracking tools work like a simple traceroute and conduct the same technique in gathering information.

  However, since packet-tracking tools have a GUI (graphical user interface), they provide a visual representation of their results. Here are three of the most popular packet-tracking tools out there: Visual Route, VisualLookout, and NeoTrace.

- MailTracking and eMailTrackerPro – Both of these tools are developed by a company called Visualware. Basically, these tools help hackers to track emails. When you use these pieces of software to modify, send, forward, or reply to an email, the succeeding tracks and actions of the original message are recorded. The sender will be notified regarding all of the actions done on the tracked message. In general, notifications are in the form of system-generated emails.

Chapter 4: How to Scan the Data You Collected

After gathering information about the target, you must perform scanning techniques. If you want the scanning stage to provide excellent results, you need to make sure that you have collected sufficient data about the system you are trying to hack. While scanning, you will continue to collect data regarding the system and each of its host systems. Data such as operating system, IP addresses, and installed applications can assist the hacker in determining the best techniques to use.

In this chapter, you will learn about three kinds of scanning:

- Vulnerability Scanning – Looks for known weaknesses inside the target network

- Port Scanning – Identifies open ports and/or services

- Network Scanning – Determines IP addresses being used in the target network or its subnets.

Let'

Th
po
to
ex
m
ha

1. The Well-Known Ports: From 0 to 1023

2. The Registered Ports: From 1024 to 49151

3. The Dynamic Ports: From 49152 to 65535

For instance, a port-scanning tool that determines port 110 as open indicates that an email server is available on that network. You should be familiar with port numbers, particularly the "well-known" ones, if you want to be a great hacker.

The Common Port Numbers

For Windows systems, the well-known port numbers are saved in C:\windows\system32\drivers\etc\services. This is a hidden file location. To see it, you have to show hidden files through the Control Panel of your computer and double-click on the filename (the file will be opened using Microsoft's Notepad). Here are the common port numbers and their corresponding applications:

- 21 – FTP (File Transfer Protocol)

- 23 – Telnet

- 80 – HTTP (Hypertext Transfer Protocol)

- 25 – SMTP (Simple Mail Transfer Protocol)

- 110 – POP3 (Post Office Protocol)

- 443 – HTTPS (HTTP Secure or HTTP over SSL)

Network Scanning

This is a process for determining the active hosts inside a system, either to test their effectiveness or exploit their weaknesses. You can identify hosts by checking their IP addresses. There are many network-scanning tools that can help you identify the live (or responding) hosts inside your target and their IP addresses.

Vulnerability Scanning

This process identifies the weaknesses of computer networks through active means. In general, hackers initiate this process by using a vulnerability scanner. This kind of scanner determines the operating system and the service packs installed in it. Afterward, the scanner determines vulnerabilities or weaknesses in the operating system's external defenses.

During the Attack Stage, the hacker can take advantage of those vulnerabilities to access confidential files or corrupt the entire system.

Additional Information About Scanning Techniques

Although scanning techniques can easily determine which hosts are active in the targeted system, it is also an easy way to get caught by the IDS (intrusion detection system). Basically, a scanning tool probes the TCP/IP ports of the system looking for IP addresses and vulnerable ports. However, intrusion detection tools can recognize these probes. Vulnerability and network scanning can be detected too, since the scanner needs to interact with the target.

The IDS of your target will detect what you are doing and flag it as a hacking activity, depending on the scanning tools you're using. Software programmers have developed a new breed of scanning tools that have different operating modes. These new scanning tools can bypass IDS and have higher chances of being undetected. As a hacker, you should collect valuable data and stay undetected.

Ping Sweep Techniques

To start the scanning stage, you should check for active systems inside the network you are going to hack. An active system is a system that responds to probes and connection requests. The most basic, although not the most precise, method to identify whether a system is active is to conduct a ping sweep for a range of IP addresses. All of the systems that will respond are considered active on the network. The ping sweep, also called ICMP (Internet Control Message Protocol) scanning, is the protocol being used to execute ping commands.

The ping sweep, or ICMP scanning, is a process in which a ping (or ICMP request) is sent throughout the network to identify the active hosts. Originally, ICMP was used as a protocol to send error and test messages between different hosts across the internet. It evolved into a testing and sweeping protocol that can be used for routers, switches, operating systems, and IP-based devices. You can use the ping command to run Echo replies and ICMP Echo requests using any IP-enabled device.

How to Use a Windows Ping

Windows operating systems have a built-in ping command that you can use to test connectivity to other networks. Here's what you need to do:

- Access the command prompt of your Windows computer.

- Enter: ping www.microsoft.com

- If the program says "Request timed out," the remote network is not working or turned off. It is also possible that the ping command was blocked. A reply, on the other hand, indicates

that the remote network is active and
responding to all ICMP requests.

How to Detect Ping Sweeps

You can use IDS (intrusion detection system) or IPS
(intrusion prevention system) to detect ping sweeps
and notify the security administrator about the
situation. Almost all proxy servers and computer
firewalls prevent ping responses so that hackers won't
know whether active systems are present in the
network.

Because of this, hackers must use other port scanning
techniques if none of the systems respond to the ping
sweep. The absence of ping responses doesn't mean
there are no active systems – it's possible that the
target is just using a ping blocker. Hackers should use
alternative identification methods. Keep in mind that
hacking requires time, persistence, and patience.

How to Scan Ports and Identify Services

Searching for available ports is the second part of the
scanning stage. Port scanning is the technique used to
search for available ports. The port scanning process
involves checking each port to identify the open ones.
In general, this type of scanning generates more

valuable data than ping sweeps about the target and its vulnerabilities.

Service determination is the third part of the scanning stage. Often, this is conducted using the tools used for scanning ports. Once the available ports have been identified, the hacker can also identify the services linked to that port number. Keep in mind the port numbers discussed earlier.

The NMAP Command Switch

Nmap is a tool that can easily and effectively perform ping sweeps, service identification, port scanning, operating system detection, and IP address detection. Nmap is a powerful tool: it can scan a large number of devices in one session. It's also supported by different operating systems such as Windows, Linux, and Unix.

The status of the port as identified by an nmap scan can be unfiltered, filtered, or open. Unfiltered means the port is closed and that no filter or firewall interferes with nmap requests. Filtered means a filter or network firewall screens the port and prevents the tool from knowing whether it is accessible. Open means the machine receives incoming nmap requests.

Chapter 5: How to Crack Passwords

In this chapter, you will learn how to crack passwords. If you know how to obtain this kind of information, you can easily hack your targets or protect your passwords from potential attackers.

The Easiest Way to Obtain a Password

In many cases, hacking attacks begin with obtaining a password to the target network. A password is an important piece of information required to access a network, and users usually choose passwords that can be guessed easily. Lots of people "recycle" passwords or select simple ones – like a childhood nickname – to assist them in remembering it. As a result of this behavior, hackers can guess a password if they have some data about the user involved. Reconnaissance and information gathering can assist hackers in guessing passwords successfully.

Different Types of Passwords

Nowadays, various types of passwords are employed to give access to networks. The characters that build a password can belong to any of these classifications:

- Numbers only

- Letters only

- Special characters only

- Numbers and letters

- Letters and special characters

- Numbers and special characters

- Numbers, letters, and special characters

Strong passwords can resist hacking attacks. Here are some tips that can help you in creating a strong password:

- ❖ It shouldn't contain any part of your name

- ❖ It should have at least eight characters

- ❖ It should contain characters from these categories:

  - o Numbers

  - o Special characters

  - o Lowercase letters

  - o Uppercase letters

Hackers may use various types of attacks to determine a password and gain access to the target. Here are some types of password attacks:

- ❖ Offline – Hybrid, Dictionary, and Brute-force approaches

❖ Active Online – Guessing the user's password. This type includes automated password determination.

❖ Passive Online – Spying on password exchanges within the target network. This type includes replay, sniffing, and man-in-the-middle attacks.

Let's discuss these attacks in detail.

Offline Attacks

These attacks require hackers to physically access a device that contains the usernames and passwords. Once the physical access is established, the hackers need to copy the username and password files onto a removable device (e.g. thumb drives). Here are three common types of offline attacks:

• Dictionary attack – Hackers consider this as the quickest and simplest form of attack. They use it to determine passwords that are actual words, which can be seen in a dictionary. In most cases, this attack utilizes a dictionary file that contains possible words. This file is encrypted through the algorithm used by the system's authentication procedure.

Since this attack assumes that the password is an actual word, it won't work against those that involve numbers or special characters.

- Hybrid attack – This is the second stage of the attack: it is used if passwords cannot be obtained using the dictionary attack. Hybrid attacks begin with a dictionary file. Then, it replaces symbols and numbers for characters that form the password. For instance, lots of users include the number "1" at the end of their password to make it stronger (or at least meet password requirements set by system administrators). Hybrid attacks are designed to find and exploit those anomalies in password creation.

- Brute-force approach – This is the most time-consuming offline attack. It tries each possible combination of symbols, numbers, lowercase letters, and uppercase letters. Since there are hundreds (or even thousands) of possible password combinations, the brute-force approach is the slowest offline attack available today.

Many hackers rely on this attack, although it consumes a large amount of time. This is because it is more effective than the two offline attacks discussed above. Since it checks every possible combination, it can identify any password if given sufficient time and computing power.

Active Online Attacks

For some people, the easiest way to gain high-level access to a network is by guessing the administrator's password. Password guessing is considered as an active form of hacking. It depends on the human behavior involved in creating passwords. However, this technique will only work on weak passwords.

How to Perform Automated Password Guessing

Hackers use automated tools to speed up the password guessing process. A simple way to automate password guessing is to utilize the shell commands of Windows computers. These commands are based on common NET USE syntax. To generate simple password-guessing scripts, do the following:

1. Use Windows' Notepad to create a username and password file. You can utilize automated tools (e.g. Dictionary Generator) to create a word list. Name the file as credentials.txt and save it in your computer's C: drive.

2. Run the FOR command to pipe this file. Here's the command you need to use:

C:\> FOR /F "token=1, 2*" %i in (credentials.txt)

3. See if you can log in to the system's hidden files by typing:

net use \\targetIP\IPC$ %i /u: %j

Passive Online Attacks

Attacks that belong to this category are referred to as "sniffing" the passwords through wired or wireless connections. In general, the target cannot detect passive attacks. Here, the password is obtained during the user verification process. The passwords acquired through this method are compared against a word list or dictionary file.

Often, account passwords are encrypted (or hashed) when submitted to the network – this is done to prevent unauthorized use and access. Since passwords are hashed or encrypted, you have to use certain tools to the break the system's algorithm.

MITM (man-in-the-middle) is a popular passive attack. Here, the hackers intercept authentication requests and forwards them to the server. Before forwarding the requests, the hackers insert a sniffer between the server and the user. A sniffer is a program that captures passwords and monitors user-to-server communications.

The replay attack is also a passive attack done online. It happens when the attackers block the password while it is on its way to the authentication server. Once the password is captured, the hackers will send authentication packets that can be used for future use. This way, the hackers don't need to crack the password or learn it through MITM. They just need to intercept the password and create authentication packets so they can access the target network later on.

How to Crack Passwords Manually

In some cases, a hacker needs to crack passwords manually. If you are in this situation, you should:

1. Search for an authorized account (e.g. Guest or Administrator)

2. Generate a list of potential passwords

3. Arrange the passwords based on their chances of successfully opening the account

4. Enter each password

5. Keep on trying until you find the correct password for the account.

Hackers may also generate a script file that enters all the passwords in a list. Although it is still considered as manual password cracking, few people use it since it is time-consuming and ineffective.

The Password Cracking Tools That You Can Use

In this section, you will learn about the different tools that you can use to obtain passwords.

- Legion – This tool automates the password-guessing process when used in NetBIOS systems. Legion does two things:

    - It checks several IP address ranges for Windows computers.

    - It provides a dictionary hacking tool that can be used manually.

- NTInfoScan – This is a scanning tool designed for NT 4.0 devices. This tool creates HTML-based reports that contain security problems discovered in the target network. Once you have this information, you can exploit your target's security issues.

- LophtCrack – This is a tool used to recover and audit passwords. It conducts SMB (Server Message Block) data captures on the target network and collects information about each login attempt. LophtCrack has hybrid, dictionary, and brute-force approach capabilities. Although Symantec has stopped developing this tool, you can still get a copy from different online sources.

- LC5 – This password cracking tool is similar to LopthCrack. That means you can use this tool if you can't download LopthCrack from any source.

- John the Ripper – This tool is in the form of a command-line. You can use it to crack both NT and Unix passwords. The broken passwords are case insensitive and might not show the actual passwords used to access the system.

How to Crack Passwords Used in Windows 2000

Windows computers have a file named "SAM." This file contains usernames and passwords used to access the computer. You will find this file in this directory: **Windows\system32\config**. You cannot access SAM file while the operating system is active: this is done to prevent hackers from copying the file. That means you cannot just turn on a Windows 2000 computer, access the file, and copy it onto your thumb drive.

To copy the SAM file, you need to boot the computer using an alternate operating system (Linux or DOS). As an additional option, you may copy this file from the computer's repair directory. If the administrator employs the RDISK capability of Windows computers to back up the network, you will find a compressed version of the SAM file in C:\windows\repair. This compressed file is named "SAM._"

You can expand this file by entering the following command into the command prompt:

C:\>expand sam._ sam

Once the SAM file has been expanded, you can use a hacking tool (e.g. LopthCrack) to run a hybrid, brute-force, or dictionary attack.

How to Use Ophcrack

If you want a newer program, you may use Ophcrack instead. Here's what you need to do to use this powerful tool:

1. Go to the webpage:
   http://ophcrack.sourceforge.net and download the program.

2. Install it into your computer.

3. Click the button that says "Load" in order to add hashes. Here are the options that you will find:

   a. *Single Hash Option* – You will manually enter the hash

   b. *PWDUMP Option* – Import a .txt file that contains the hashes you want to load

   c. *Encrypted SAM Option* – Extract the hash from the SAM and SYSTEM files

   d. *Local SAM Option* – Dump the SAM file from the machine you are currently using

   e. *Remote SAM Option* – Dump the SAM file through a remote computer

4. Click the button that says "Tables."

5. Click on the buttons that say "Enable."

6. Set the rainbow tables using the up and down arrows. You can speed up this procedure by saving the rainbow tables on a fast storage (e.g. a hard disk).

7. Start the cracking procedure by clicking on the button that says "Crack." Click on the "Save" button if you want to store the results you have received.

Chapter 6: Backdoors and Trojans

In this chapter, you will learn about the two techniques used by hackers to access their targets. Study this material carefully since it will provide you with detailed explanations, instructions, and tips.

Backdoors and Trojans

Backdoors and Trojans are kinds of malicious software employed to attack and infect computer networks.

Backdoors

A backdoor is a computer program or a group of related programs that an attacker installs on a target network to secure future access. In general, hackers install backdoor so they can access their target/s anytime they want. Once this undetectable access is established, the attacker may hack the network further and obtain other pieces of information.

Usually, hackers disguise backdoor programs by offering free stuff online. Before installing the backdoor, hackers should study the system to discover the things that they can offer. As you can see, you should gather information about your target before using the actual hacking techniques.

Hackers often provide new programs or services to trick system administrators. To make sure that this technique won't be detected, attackers give their services or programs inconspicuous names. Also, they use programs that are manually activated or completely disabled.

This strategy is effective since system administrators often search for "weird" things in the network whenever a hacking attempt happens. That means the backdoor technique is effective and efficient – the hacker can access the network with the least amount of tracks in the activity logs. The "backdoored" program or service allows the hacker to obtain high-level access rights – in some cases, even that of a system administrator.

RATs (Remote Access Trojans) are a type of backdoors employed to allow remote access to a compromised network. They provide practical functions to the victim and, meanwhile, open a network port on the machine being used. Once started, the RAT will behave like an .exe file and interact with the computer's Registry keys – these keys are responsible for the system services and booting procedures. Unlike ordinary backdoors, RATs connect themselves to the computer's operating system and often come in two files: the server file and the client file. The server file is planted on the hacked machine, and the client file is used by the hacker to manipulate the network.

In general, RATs allow hackers to control the target network anytime they want. Actually, one of the signs that a network has been attacked is uncommon behavior on the network (e.g. pop-up windows suddenly appearing even if the system is idle).

Trojans

Trojans are malicious programs disguised as harmless ones. In most cases, Trojans appear to conduct useful functions for the victim but actually enable hackers to access the computer network. Attackers often place Trojans inside software packages and offer them as free downloads through online sources. Once installed, a Trojan will steal or destroy data, and sometimes cause system slowdowns or crashes. You can also use Trojans to launch other hacking attacks, like a DDoS (Distributed Denial of Service).

Hackers use Trojans to manipulate files, manage processes, run commands, capture keystrokes, view screen images, and shutdown or restart infected computers. Modern Trojans can link themselves to their source or announce the attack using an IRC (Internet Relay Chat).

Here are some of the avenues you can use to send a Trojan to a victim's device:

- Internet Relay Chat

- Email attachment

- IM (Instant Messenger) attachment

- Downloadable Internet program or file

- File sharing through NetBIOS

Different Kinds of Trojans

Here are the different types of Trojans being used today:

Destructive Trojans – These are used to corrupt or erase files on a network.

Proxy Trojans – These are used to create a new attacking avenue or launch attacks to other networks.

FTP Trojans – These are used to create FTP servers that can copy files onto a network.

DOS Trojans – These are used to execute a denial-of-service hacking attack.

Security Disabler Trojans – These are used to disable antivirus programs.

The Most Popular Trojans Used by Hackers

Expert hackers have their own favorites when it comes to malwares. The following list will show you the most powerful Trojans being used by modern hackers.

- TROJ_QAZ – This is a hacking tool that changes the name of the notepad.exe application to note.com. Then, it will name itself as notepad.exe and save itself onto the Windows computer. This kind of Trojan is launched whenever the user opens a Notepad. It has backdoor capabilities that hackers can use to link to and manipulate computers using the 7597 port.

- Tini – This is a small Trojan program designed for Windows computers. It spies on the 7777 port and allows the hacker to send commands to the target network. A hacker needs to telnet to the 7777 port in order to use a Tini Trojan.

- Netcat – This Trojan opens UDP or TCP ports on the target network using a command-line user interface. The hacker may link to those ports (using a telnet) and access the compromised network. Here's what you need to do if you want to use Netcat:

    o Download the Netcat program and install it on your computer. There are lots of Netcat versions for machines that run on Windows – you can easily get them online. In addition, you can use Netcat for Unix computers since this tool was originally designed for that operating system.

    o You should run this program on both the server and the client.

o For the server part of the connection, run the following command:

nc −L −p 123 −t −e cmd.exe

o For the client, run this command:

nc <the server's IP address> <the server's listening port>

o After running those commands, you'll see a command prompt window in the Netcat client.

Chapter 7: How to Hack Wireless Networks

This chapter will teach you how to access networks that rely on wireless (or Wi-Fi) connections.

Using a Wireless Sniffer to Identify SSIDs

A usual attack on wireless networks involves sniffing or eavesdropping. This attack is easy to perform and often occurs at Wi-Fi hotspots or any installation access point. The reason for this is simple – data packets are sent unencrypted inside the wireless networks. With unencrypted WLANs, you can capture passwords for SMTP, POP3, and FTP protocols then save them in cleartext form.

Here's what you need to do:

1. Go to www.wildpackets.com and download the Omnipeek program.

Important Note: You should have an Omnipeek-supported wireless network adapter if you want to capture data packets properly. Access the www.wildpackets.com website and see the supported network adapters of the Omnipeek program.

2. Run the program and click on the button that says "New Capture."

3. Choose your wireless adapter from the list.

Important Note: In the adapter section, the WildPackets API should say "Yes" or the adapter won't work as it should.

4. Click on the tab that says "802.11" and scan all available channels. Later on, once you have determined a particular wireless network, you may select its SSID to capture traffic from that network.

5. Hit "OK" to begin the capture. A new window will display the frames that have been captured. You can double-click on those frames if you want to view more details.

6. Once you are satisfied with the amount of captured frames, click on the "Stop" button. Click on the "Display" button and choose POP from the dropdown menu. That option will display email frames only. If you want to see other frames, just click on the "Display" button again and choose your preferred frame. Here are the frames that you can capture using Omnipeek: FTP, POP, HTTP, TELNET, and SMTP.

You will get valuable network information (e.g. passwords) from these frames.

7. If you want to find available APs (Access Points) and Stations, click on the WLAN button. Omnipeek's WLAN screen will show you the following information:

- SSID

- Channel

- STA MAC

- BSSID

Access points that don't broadcast their SSID will be shown as "00x0." That code will be displayed until Omnipeek identifies the SSID of those access points. As soon as the SSID is identified, the information will be shown in the program's WLAN screen.

Conclusion

I hope this book was able to help you in learning about different hacking techniques and procedures.

The next step is to practice your hacking skills by attacking test computers or networks.

Finally, if you enjoyed this book, then I'd like to ask you for a favor, would you be kind enough to leave a review for this book on Amazon? It'd be greatly appreciated!

Thank you and good luck!

Printed in Great Britain
by Amazon